# UNHINGED

## Poems by
## Sharon Charde

BLUE LIGHT PRESS ◆ 1ST WORLD PUBLISHING

SAN FRANCISCO ◆ FAIRFIELD ◆ DELHI

*UNHINGED*

Copyright ©2019 by Sharon Charde

1st World Library
PO Box 2211
Fairfield, IA 52556
www.1stworldpublishing.com

Blue Light Press
www.bluelightpress.com
bluelightpress@aol.com

Book & Cover Design
Melanie Gendron
melaniegendron999@gmail.com

Cover Art
"Foray" by Jane Sangerman
jmsangerman@gmail.com
www.janesangerman.com

Author Photo
Joanna Eldredge Morrissey

First Edition

ISBN 978-1-4218-3631-7

*To my past*

# TABLE OF CONTENTS

# TO MYSELF AT TWENTY

Don't do it, girl, you'll
disappear into what you can't
understand. It's just one
page, this tiny unlived
life you're stepping into.
Still no one's mother, you
haven't yet loved too
much, you don't know
the art of sorrow. Who
you might have been
doesn't haunt, the necklace
that almost strangled is
still in the box. There's
purity in this aloneness.
Pay the entrance fee
before your scream
is screamed, while
your son's death only
exists in your husband's
dream. Nancy's daughter
will never have to ask
if you'll be happy again.
Send in a replacement.
back away fast. Hurry,
girl, it's what you don't
do that saves you.

## AFTER THIRTY YEARS

Loss, we'd like you to be quiet, not
shouted out like the emperor peonies
burning red in my garden, the pink
ones wild on the lawn. Can't you be
more like prayer, a dimmed chandelier,
sheer silk on a mannequin? You don't
listen, sweep in to tango in the room
I've just managed to empty. Pretending
to be demure as the Virgin Mary, I
steal a blue veil, long white dress,
shiver thin-skinned in a corner, think
about how God always gives us more
than we can handle.

# ROME, AGAIN

I still can't get over what Raffa told us about the animals, how
they were bred to be shredded for people's amusement. Elephants,
giraffes, tigers, she shows us the dungeons where they were kept,
where the gladiators fed them, then led them to slaughter. Too
much death here, haven't I noticed it before? The Pieta, the
Caravaggios, the Catacombs, Coliseum, all the sarcophagi in
churches, our son. On the plane coming over I'd thought every
teenager in Boston was on his way to Rome. With their green
tour tee-shirts, plugged-in ears, backpacks, and hoodies, they
swarmed us with clamor, cell phones, candy wrappers. A skinny
boy next to me fell asleep against my arm. We've brought our
grandson, another return to touch the bruise this city's given us.
Something's different this time though I'm not sure what. Emma
takes us to the Vatican early so we can see the colors of God
without the crowds. After green risotto at Hostaria Costanza she
leaves us to wander Campo de Fiori, bring yellow roses to the
Tiber wall. We stroll up Via Del Corso, ride the elevator to the
top of the Wedding Cake. Our grandson is cranky. I think he'd
rather be on the tour with the teens. We begin to drink vino rosso
at lunch, get cranky too. I suggest a picnic in Piazza Del Populo.
But what he wants are souvenirs, selfies, Facetime with his family.
Maybe to get away from our grief? I want to get away from it
too, lasso my life to a more merciful anchor. Rome, your arm too
heavy on my shoulder. *Per piacere*, let me go.

# CATACOMBS

The third time, I didn't want to
go, cold underground hollows
damp and dripping. Loss had already
put me in my place. So Francesco drove
them, then came to find me, told
of the other boy cut into pieces
by the train, the troubles over it.
Shady that afternoon in the Aventine
under the jacaranda trees, so many years
later. After, I walked to the wall you fell from,
fatigued with remembering. No music
has been written for this country yet,
ache of pilgrimage made too many times.
I guess I'll have to do it.

# FILAMENT

snowing   all day   no one      shovels a path      tomorrow
it will be   sunshine      no way to tell   what's next   death
a  place   to arrive     and leave from         how to familiarize
yourself     with this        stay away              from the door
to the  unfurnished    room     *I'm that close*   irregular
adagio    in the wreckage  half-erased       follow   the song
can you                    follow                       the song

# WHAT IT'S LIKE, NOW

Life: a problem of what to do. I hadn't taken notes and I should have.
Halo around razors of its days, how could I have known such ravage
would come? Lavish gift of quotidian malice. Or maybe not malice,
but just what was given in the handouts ordinary humans get. Why
would I be special? *Come on. You're strong, you can take it,* they
told me. I bought another black dress, definitely meant for someone
younger. Silk, knee-length, ruffle on one shoulder, off the other one,
it showed too much of me, It wasn't sad enough. But I didn't return it.

# HUNGRY GHOST

I know her well, the never-enough
girl, pushing her pinhole mouth
out for more, body a rental space
for the blizzard of yearning
she drags around daily. Longing
for what was not had felt so right,
appetite she could not step back
from. I wanted to tell you the tenant
was evicted but just now Susie took
my picture and I hunger to scrape
the flesh from my chin, the spots
from my cheeks, thin out my legs,
re-do my hair. I really do look as old
as I am. This morning I told Rikki
that all I wanted was to be whole,
but now I'm ready to rush out
to Gap for a new jacket, Godiva
for more dark chocolate.

# BIRD

I'd wanted something, I admit. But then
I'd been wanting something so long I was
accustomed to that tired fire, a chubby
Italian girl praying to be pretty, the mother
who longed her dead son alive. Maybe
being single would be better, planting more
dahlias could make the garden grander?
Only last month I told Ellen I wished
my husband were a woman. Will I always
be one who wants to leap from the chair
as soon as I sit? Asia, another pilgrimage.
I plunge into the throngs, raising my arm
to cross the streets where no one stops, see
karst from sampans, feed monks rice. I
buy a black bird in a small straw cage, climb
234 steps to set it free. "Forgive yourself,
forgive others," the tour guide tells us
to say, so I do, flinging it into the Laotian
sky. Little bird, such large work.

# RESHUFFLE

What a well I fell into
this morning, a door
in the wind, doubt
without faith, all that
childhood inside me.
Isn't there something
in us that can forget?
When love is over,
its ashy bits scattered,
we should stop wanting
all the things that never
happened, praying
sorrowful mysteries
again and again. I have
scissors, a knife, don't use
them. God of the ravaged,
do what they could do.

# HOSTAGE

My son's old friend Fred wants
to know if poets ever write about
joy. *Not much*, I say, *it's hard.*
And death is always so close —
sometimes I think of throwing
myself under the UPS truck when
I'm walking my dog.  It's not that
I want to die, it's just that I've
devoted my life to unhappiness.
Replacing myself would be tough.
I'd have to dump rotting leftovers
from the back of the fridge, clean
all the closets, reset the clocks,
rinse his death from my neurons,
carve out my losses with hatchets
and knives. Wreckage would be
everywhere. No more stations
of the cross. And without hunger
for catastrophe, tomorrow could
devour me. How could love be
love if it's easy?

# WHAT I SAVE

the clothes my son died in
shoes I haven't worn in ten years
*I love you* when there is no *I love you*
our breath

# TOUGH COOKIE

That's what Simone called
me, she said it twice,
*you're one tough cookie* —
does it show that much?
I'd thought my disguise
acceptable, black turtleneck,
jeans like anyone would wear,
even glasses. Though I do
lay down heavy declarations,
love like a knife, axe the exes.
Tough cookie. Bite into me
and break your teeth, does she
mean that? I think I'd at least
like to be soft enough to be
swallowed.

# SPASMS

So many times I've wanted to leave
our life. Fell back. Money. What
people would say. Safety. Our son.
Erasure.  Second husband, second wife.
You let things be, I want to keep moving.
You care about the kale you picked, I
care about the grass growing. *Wait*, that's
your mantra. *The body will heal itself.*
Maybe it can't, maybe it hasn't. Peter
asked last night, *where won't you go?*
Here. To why I've never left, why you
haven't, even though you threw a wineglass
at the wall that night I went to meet Tony.
I want to be a wife, I don't want to be a wife.
It's easier to write about death than life.
Sometimes our bond seems so fragile
a butterfly's wing could break it. What
I haven't been haunts me. We were too
young. Our fault he died, a marriage
mixed with truth and lies. Yesterday I met
a skunk in the woods, thought of how it
would be if she sprayed me, I'd never get
rid of the scent. Palimpsest of us if I'd left.
Maybe other women are braver. Place I won't
go? The one without you.

# WHITE

is holy and I am
not, child's mouth
opens for the Bridegroom
to enter and He does
not, bones of white
picked clean by grief
and the easing
of grief, too naked
here, too human
and lonely, too
simple, too loud,
white, let there be
less light, there is too
much of you, half-
life of might, scenery
of sorrow, stain
of love, white, thread
your needle, push
through death's tithe
to the other side, ravage
the black, excite

# PRAYER

All I want is to sit here naked
on my narrow bed, without
mishaps, wrong turns, losses
and longings stamping their feet
on the floor around me. Last
year, I would have liked someone
beside me, stroking my nipple,
ease of skin on skin. But that was
only trouble. Just now I can't
bear that history, that wall
of sorrow, the greed to soothe
my bruises. Someone said *there
is no greater blasphemy against
God than the refusal of happiness.*
I don't want to refuse it but I do.
Why is joy such a taboo? I want
not to want. I want not to think
of how everyone's got cancer or
being shot. My mother wants me
to tell her what a good mother
she was, but I don't. Why can't I
loosen her teeth, give her that lie
to take to her dying? I want to
leave this line of thinking, feel
tenderness for the lost. Instead
I switch subjects, fix dinner, place
a top on the pot of our simmering.

# NOT ME, THE OTHER MOTHERS SAY

Now, death is everywhere, the daily
news, the mulberry tree collapsed
in the last storm, my mother's breath.
I've survived for this? Loss like
those trick candles that never
blow out, I might have gotten them
for his birthday once. Make a wish
but it could never come true.
Listen: keep the door to grief
unlocked.

# UNHINGED

In love with damage so long
today I swallowed flowers,
foraged leaves, sipped a soup
so green it shone. Across
the street a temple, chanting
monks. Later I will go inside,
drop sticks for a fortune. #3
it says, but the message box
is empty. No dead son, bad
wife, just a small unoccupied
wooden square. The anxious
tour guide offers another fate.
*You will be a queen this year,*
*have good luck, much money,*
*if you have a daughter, same*
*for her.* But I prefer the empty
box. *Look*, it says, *start over.*
*Start.*

# HEAVY BEAT

You have a next. Next year, next child,
next job, next house, next husband, wife,
girlfriend. Next thing on the list. Keep
going, keep moving, keep searching. It's
all a quest for you. My next is supposed
to be review. I've been a woman for a long time,
nothing shining is going to strike me now.
Loss, strapped to my body like an anchor,
demands to be examined, makes me
note what I've done and haven't, how I've
tried to walk evenly on uneven ground,
failed almost all the time. *Thank you*
*for not leaving me,* we say to each other
on our fifty-second anniversary. Let's imagine
there is tenderness for the rest, tulips
the deer don't eat, summers still of ripe tomatoes,
cut grass, that rocky beach, growing old,
the persistence of its heavy beat.

# THE GLASS IS ALREADY BROKEN

You want to sit out in the rain, I want to come in.
Laughing, I say now you would fall in love with someone
who was willing to get wet with you. Would she be
the black-haired desk clerk in Santa Pau, the cute waitress
at Manna Dew, a friend of our son's? No, you're not
one of those men who marry the young. Besides,
you'd never leave me, your quotidian fuse. I didn't
belong to my life before I met you, then I belonged
to yours. Nietzsche says the body is a big sagacity. Mine
knows its long song, its wrong notes, democracy
of blame, ordinary grace. Its need to draw lines
between us. Last night, when you wanted to drive,
I felt our clamped knot tighten. As you packed the car
with the things that would take me away from you —
sweaters enough for two weeks, bags of books and pens —
I wondered when the real leaving would happen, as it will.
You tell me you'll die before me, you're sure of it. We
leave so we can stay. We stay so we can leave, when it pours
and we are both without the choice.

# EVANESCENCE

The past is nailed shut. I can never hold
the room as I once did with my body, long
shiny hair. That absence will stay, as
it should. Mess of youth, its long necklace
of regrets, crossed wires sending out restless
flares, more blood than bone. Most of my
life is over. So much time on thin ice
prepared me for becoming someone I might
love, though a thirst that never got slaked
lurks like old perfume.

# DON'T READ THIS

I'm only going to tell you it will
all fall apart. Everything you love
will be taken from you. Don't believe
it? Look at me, clinging to a vine about
to break from a cliff. A son's a son
till he takes a wife, husband, sure
he'll die before me, other son already
has. You're praying to the wrong god,
if you think he'll help. I'd try another,
she'll know the real deal. Get smart.
Let go of that vine.

# LAST CALL

I want to be terrific again. I want
  to stride into a room, be important,
not some elderly mannequin, senior
citizen stained with aging. I want
my colors back. I'd like you to believe
in me, even the hungriest and ugliest
parts. The other night, I cried like a baby
cries, from the feet up, my whole body
sobbed. So much is wrong with the world.
I'm just learning how I love the fire
though it doesn't keep me from being
cold. But even shivering in my thinned
skin, I still think the life I have is
the one worth living in.

# WHILE THERE IS STILL TIME

All our friends look so old, some a little
bent over, others bald, developing quavers,
cancers, cataracts. Taking daily naps. I
know we look nothing like them, we are
only the age we met at, believing everything,
unknowing of loss, distance,  how one story
becomes another, how promises falter,
questions get noisier. We always knew
what to do next. Remember? Have a baby,
buy a house, plant a garden, get a dog, bury
a son. I'd thought you were proof against
drowning, you'd thought I was. Costumed
as adults, we continued our fictions, until
we couldn't. Out here now on the fringes
of the end, I'm too tired to pretend. As our
deaths are trying on their suits and dresses,
let's be kind, while there is still time.

## ODE TO DEATH

You gave me no time-outs, dear death. No
way to stop being everything but what I
was to all the edges. No noticing anything
but what was right there, in front, in back,
underneath, on top of me. Restricted to your
greedy snare, I couldn't move, had no prayer
to pull me out, no *god wanted him* or *he's
another angel now,* to soothe. *Only the good
die young* left me comfortless, time hasn't
healed. I can still peel the scab away, feel
your raw wound. Such purity, to feel only
pain. I don't blame you anymore, you
happen every day to everyone, why not
my son? Death, you've offered me a kind
of peace. I'm unable to return to the place
I was before you came. Separated from others
who don't know you yet, I stand alone. *You're
too sad for me,* people say. You give me solitude.
You give me singularity, a kind of dignity I'd
never have if not for you. Death, I've paid
your  dowry, we're married now.

# ABOUT THE AUTHOR

Sharon Charde is not only a poet. A family therapist, a former shaman-in-training, a volunteer writing teacher to delinquent girls in a residential treatment facility, a minimally competent carpenter and devoted yoga practitioner, she is a veteran of fifty-five years of marriage to the same man. Her life as wife, mother and grandmother informs her poems as well as a memoir that will come out next year. She has been published widely in literary journals, including *Poet Lore, Upstreet, Rattle, Calyx* and *Ping Pong,* and has one full-length poetry collection, *Branch In His Hand,* as well as four prize-winning chapbooks and many award-winning poems. *Four Trees From Ponte Sisto,* an hour-long radio drama shaped from her poems was broadcast by the BBC in 2012. She currently continues to teach the women's writing retreats she developed twenty-five years ago and has been leading ever since. Charde has been awarded fellowships to The Corporation Of Yaddo, The MacDowell Colony, Virginia Center For The Creative Arts and Vermont Studio Center.

## ACKNOWLEDGMENTS

Thanks to *Mudfish,* 21, summer 2019 for publishing "Evanescence."

And thanks to my many outstanding poetry mentors for all their teaching and support during the last thirty years: Sharon Olds, Brenda Hillman, Marie Howe, Ellen Bass, Honor Moore, Eileen Myles and of course, Natalie Goldberg, who began it all.

Much appreciation to Jane Sangerman for "Foray,"and Jo Eldredge Morrissey for photographic skills par excellence.

Deep gratitude and love to my husband John, who has been the inspiration, for better or for worse, for many of these poems.

And I bow down to to The MacDowell Colony, Yaddo, Virginia Center For the Creative Arts and Vermont Studio Center, where most of these poems were written.

## OTHER BOOKS BY SHARON CHARDE

*Branch In His Hand*

*Bad Girl At The Altar Rail*

*Four Trees Down From Ponte Sisto*

*After Blue*

*Incendiary*

CPSIA information can be obtained
at www.ICGtesting.com
Printed in the USA
BVHW031219210719
554004BV00001B/155/P

9 781421 836317